· PEOPLES *of* NORTH AMERICA ·

Iroquois

STEVE POTTS

CREATIVE EDUCATION · CREATIVE PAPERBACKS

BUFFALO, N.Y.

Published by Creative Education and Creative Paperbacks
P.O. Box 227, Mankato, Minnesota 56002
Creative Education and Creative Paperbacks
are imprints of The Creative Company
www.thecreativecompany.us

Design and production by Christine Vanderbeek
Art direction by Rita Marshall
Printed in the United States of America

Photographs by Alamy (Lebrecht Music and Arts Photo Library, North Wind Picture Archives,
nsf, Photoshot Holdings Ltd, PRISMA ARCHIVO, Philip Scalia, Stock Montage Inc., ZUMA Press
Inc.), Corbis (Nathan Benn/Ottochrome, Bettmann, Blue Lantern Studio, Corbis, Lebrecht
Music & Arts, Miguel Juarez Lugo/ZUMA Press, David Muench, Swim Ink, Tarker, Marilyn
Angel Wynn/Nativestock Pictures), Dreamstime (Saladorec), iStockphoto (foofie, ihoe),
Shutterstock (OHishiapply, satit_srihin, stockelements, Transia Design, Michiel de Wit),
SuperStock (Newberry Library, Stock Connection)

Library of Congress Cataloging-in-Publication Data
Potts, Steve.
Iroquois / Steve Potts.
p. cm. — (Peoples of North America) • Includes bibliographical references and index.
Summary: A history of the people and events that influenced the North American Indian
confederacy known as the Iroquois, including Chief Hiawatha and conflicts such as the
American Revolution.
ISBN 978-1-60818-552-8 (hardcover)
ISBN 978-1-62832-153-1 (pbk)
1. Iroquois Indians—History—Juvenile literature.
2. Iroquois Indians—Social life and customs—Juvenile literature. I. Title.

E99.I7P678 2014
974.7004'9755—dc23   2014041746

CCSS: RI.5.1, 2, 3, 5, 6, 8, 9; RH.6-8.4, 5, 6, 7, 8, 9

HC 9 8 7 6 5 4 3 2
First Edition PBK 9 8 7 6 5 4 3 2 1

6420

PEOPLES *of* NORTH AMERICA

Iroquois

STEVE POTTS

CREATIVE EDUCATION • CREATIVE PAPERBACKS

Table of Contents

THE SENECA CHIEF CORNPLANTER (ON PAGE 3);
CEREMONIAL ITEMS (PICTURED HERE)

Introduction

Still viewed today as one of America's most beautiful regions, northern New York was home a thousand years ago to five Indian nations that hunted in its rolling hills, fished in its many rivers and lakes, and farmed its fertile soil. This environment of the eastern woodlands provided food and shelter for the Oneida, Onondaga, Seneca, Mohawk, and Cayuga. Known in historic times as the Iroquois, those five nations (and later a sixth, the Tuscarora) came to play an important role in the history of what would become the United States.

The *Haudenosaunee*, as the Iroquois call themselves, are often referred to as the "People of the **LONGHOUSE**." This name was given to them to show how important their dwellings were to their culture. The ancestors of the Iroquois spread across northern New York as early as A.D. 1000. They developed a culture that revolved around farming. Within two centuries of their first contact with Europeans, the Iroquois became embroiled in wars between European powers and were fighting to hold on to their ancestral lands. By the end of the American Revolution in 1783, the Iroquois, like many Indian nations, found themselves directly in the path of persistent westward-moving settlers. As time went on and their lands were gradually overtaken, the Iroquois struggled to maintain their culture. Their story is one of the most fascinating in all of American history.

THE MOHAWK LIVED NEAR HEART LAKE, CLOSE TO THE TOWN OF LAKE PLACID, IN THE ADIRONDACKS.

· IROQUOIS ·

From East to West

PEOPLES *of* NORTH AMERICA

Archaeological discoveries and Iroquois oral history traditions show that the Iroquois culture originated in the area around the St. Lawrence River, Lake Simcoe in Ontario, and the Susquehanna River. By A.D. 1000, the ancestors of today's Iroquois were growing corn in New York. Six hundred years later, historians believe there were approximately 15,000 Iroquois living in the eastern woodlands.

From the 1500s to 1722, when the Tuscarora joined the Iroquois Confederacy, the Haudenosaunee were arranged from west to east across northern New York. The Mohawk were on the easternmost end and the Seneca were westernmost, with the Oneida, Onondaga, and Cayuga spread out between. Each nation had its own customs and language, and each exercised control over its respective area.

Referred to as the "Keepers of the Western Door," the Seneca were likely the most numerous tribe of Haudenosaunee and occupied villages between the Genesee River and Canandaigua Lake. Thanks to military campaigns that extended their reach to present-day northwestern Pennsylvania, the Seneca were powerful but often faced opposition from another local tribe, the Huron. They (and every other nation requiring materials for making tools) traded

A MOHAWK LEADER WHO WAS GRANDFATHER TO JOSEPH BRANT WAS AN EARLY FRIEND OF THE BRITISH IN THE 1700S.

with the Mohawk, who called themselves "People of the Flint Place" and were also known as "Keepers of the Eastern Door."

Based in the Mohawk Valley of eastern New York, the Mohawk had access to rivers that connected the Great Lakes with the Atlantic Ocean. Such a location brought them in contact with various tribes and, later, European traders. The Oneida of central New York were immediate neighbors. Self-identified as "People of the Standing Stone" (from an ancient story involving the ability to shape-shift into stones to avoid an enemy), the Oneida were organized into three clans, or family groups: Wolf, Turtle, or Bear.

Between the Oneida and Cayuga were the Onondaga, the most centrally located Iroquoian tribe. Like the middle of a longhouse, where fires burned to warm the interior, the Onondaga were later considered the "Keepers of the Fire" among the Haudenosaunee. And it was in Onondaga territory that members of the Iroquois Confederacy would meet to discuss laws and other government business. West of the Onondaga settlements lay the Cayuga

⟶ **THE MOST FAMOUS IROQUOIS** ⟵ *The American poet Henry Wadsworth Longfellow published "The Song of Hiawatha" in 1855. Although the poem had nothing to do with the historical figure of Hiawatha, it did publicize the name of this important Iroquois political leader. The poem's commercial success also guaranteed that hundreds of towns, lakes, schools, and trains would be named after Hiawatha.*

R.A.Grider
1897.

A COLORFUL HISTORY *The Iroquois, like most Indian nations, did not have a writing system. To aid in their teaching and memory, they used visual reminders such as bead* **WAMPUM**. *Different-colored beads were sewn onto leather belts with designs that represented important events (as shown opposite). Tribal elders memorized the events symbolized by the belts so that, if called upon, they could recount the stories. The belts were stored in the largest Onondaga village and were looked after by the wampum keeper.*

homeland, in the Finger Lakes region of modern upstate New York.

The various peoples made use of seasonal foods (gathering nuts, berries, and other wild produce) and cultivated corn, beans, and squash. The fish abundant in lakes, rivers, and streams were expertly caught, and hunters sought game in the forests. Trees such as sap-bearing elms lent their bark to make trays and bowls used in preparing foods and transporting water.

Constantly competing for resources and living in close proximity, the tribes grew skilled in warfare rather than negotiation. Some possibly engaged in cannibalism, or eating human flesh. Gradually, the tribal warfare became so widespread and so many people died that the tribes looked for ways to encourage peace.

Oral history passed down through the generations tells the story of how the five tribes came together. Scholars think the confederacy could have formed as early as the 12th century or as late as 1451. According to the traditional account, there was a Huron (or perhaps Onondaga) Indian named **DEGANAWIDA**, often referred to simply as "The Great Peacemaker." Deganawida spread a message of peace and order, promoting a plan that involved 13 laws. Ayenwatha (Hiawatha), an Onondaga leader who had been

· IROQUOIS ·

Bound by Clan

PEOPLES *of* NORTH AMERICA

The Iroquois lifestyle revolved around home, family, and farming. For homes, the Iroquois used the longhouse, a large struc-
ture designed to hold an extended family of several generations.
Longhouses were built by bending trees down into a frame, tying them
together with sinew (cords made from animal skins), and covering the frame
with bark stripped from trees. Men cut down young trees and made a frame.
Women stripped elm bark and flattened it into shingles. A path was made
down the center of each house, and a smoke hole and fire pit were placed
about every 20 feet (6.1 m). Inside, large baskets held food and clothing, while
tools and weapons hung on hooks fixed to the walls and ceiling. Wooden platforms near the bottom of the walls were covered with animal skins and fur
robes. These platforms were used as chairs during the day and beds at night.

The Iroquois family usually consisted of a father, mother, children, and
often the mother's sisters and their families. Grandparents were typically
also part of the extended family. The Iroquois were a matrilineal society. For
them, that meant that when a man married, he moved in with his wife's family. A woman and her mother, sisters, and daughters worked together while
they farmed—the main task of Iroquois women—and it made sense not to split

REPLICAS OF 15TH-CENTURY LONGHOUSES GIVE MOD-
ERN PEOPLE THE OPPORTUNITY TO STEP INTO HISTORY.

A FENCE OF TALL
WOODEN STAKES
(KNOWN AS A
PALISADE) SERVED
AS AN INITIAL LINE
OF DEFENSE FOR A
VILLAGE.

up the women in the family when they married. Men hunted and often went to war with neighboring tribes. They then brought war captives home with them. These captives were often adopted into the community.

Iroquois villages were often large, consisting of 15 to 20 longhouses, and were sometimes fortified against enemy attack with walls and fences. People lived in the longhouses and went outside the village to cultivate the fields. Farming was based on three crops—corn, beans, and squash—native to the Americas. These crops, known as the "Three Sisters," were harvested each fall and stored in pits dug in the ground beneath the floor of the longhouse. The importance of the Three Sisters was once described by Chief Lewis Farmer in the following way: "We plant them together, three kinds of seeds in one hole. They want to be together with each other, just as we Indians want to be together with each other. So long as the Three Sisters are with us, we know we will never starve."

Iroquois women used a hill-planting system for their crops. Seeds or kernels were buried in holes. After young plants sprouted, the soil would be mounded around the seedlings. Each hill would reach a height of about a foot (30.5 cm) and be two feet (61 cm) wide. Rows between hills were measured by human footsteps and were usually only one step apart. A hill where corn was planted was also used to plant beans. As the beans grew, they used the corn

Being Iroquois

⇒ **MAKING PEACE WITH THE SETTLERS** ⇐ *The Dutch and later the English made treaties called covenants with the Iroquois. After several covenants were made, the series of agreements was called the Covenant Chain. The first agreement in this chain was made in Albany, New York, between the Dutch and Iroquois in 1677. These agreements helped set up trade between the Europeans and Iroquois. They also helped gain Iroquois support during wars the Europeans fought with each other in North America.*

stalk as a pole for support. There was enough space between the rows to plant squash, whose leaves trapped moisture that helped all Three Sisters.

In addition to farming, the Iroquois continued their ancient practice of gathering fruits, vegetables, nuts, and herbs from the surrounding forests. Their diet also included several kinds of fish, along with meat from ducks, geese, and deer. Iroquois men were skilled with the bow and arrow. Boys learned how to hunt when they were young.

Each family in an Iroquois longhouse represented a different clan. Clans were named after animals, perhaps following the pattern of the Oneida and Mohawk, which have only the three basic clans common to each nation (Bear, Turtle, and Wolf). Other Iroquois nations had more clans, but the clans were held in common among all villages within that nation. The Iroquois believed that the spirits of these animals protected the clan.

The oldest woman of a clan was known as the clan mother. She owned most clan property and gave her family name to clan members. She chose the men who would lead the clan. These men became members of the tribal council, which made important decisions on behalf of the nation. The tribal council in turn chose members of the Grand Council, a body that met in late summer or early fall of each year. Every Iroquois adult, including women, had a say in government decisions. When the women's rights movement began in the U.S. in the 1830s, its leaders, such as Susan B. Anthony, used the Iroquois as an example of a society in which

Like the Iroquois, other nearby tribes such as the Huron and Ojibwa lived in longhouses and/or wigwams.

women and men held more equal roles and shared participation.

Clan decisions were made by consensus, or common agreement. Clan leaders consulted with the clan mother and other clan
members and took their advice before making final decisions. Clan
leaders could be removed from their leadership posts if they went
against the advice or will of the majority of their clan.

The Iroquois practiced what came to be known as the longhouse religion. They believed in a Creator who made all things in
nature, so the Iroquois thanked the Creator in their rituals and
ceremonies. The Iroquois also believed in the presence of spirits
in all living things. Some spirits were good. Others were bad. The
Iroquois wore masks made from basswood trees to scare away the
evil spirits of sickness and disease as they performed healing rituals. The False Face Society continues to wear dramatic wooden

━━⊶ **BRITAIN'S IROQUOIS ALLY** ⊷━━ *As a young man, Joseph Brant (Thayendanegea) became close friends with William Johnson, the official British representative to the Iroquois. Johnson arranged for Brant to attend school in Connecticut to learn English. During the Revolution, Brant sided with the British and led raids that destroyed many New York farms. When the war ended in 1783, Brant and other Mohawk still loyal to Britain settled in Ontario and founded the town of Brantford, where their descendants live today.*

masks in its medicinal rituals.

Some ceremonies were based on the Iroquois calendar, which had 13 moons, or months. In January or February, the midwinter ceremony took place five days after the midwinter new moon appeared. The ceremony began with men in masks (called "Big Heads") running through the longhouses and stirring up ashes in the fires. This invited everyone to participate in the dancing, feasting, and games that followed as part of the nine-day celebration. Dream-guessing was also part of the midwinter ceremony. Dreamers came to each longhouse and shared their dreams. People would guess what these dreams meant.

No matter when a ceremony took place, most had themes of renewal, healing, and thanksgiving in common. Several ceremonies were centered on agricultural practices such as planting and harvest, and others were specific to a food crop, such as strawberries or maize (corn). In everything, the Iroquois gave thanks to the Great Spirit.

AFTER LEARNING TO READ AND WRITE ENGLISH, JOSEPH BRANT BECAME INTERESTED IN TRANSLATING TEXTS INTO THE MOHAWK LANGUAGE.

When the French arrived in Canada in the early 1600s, life began to change for the Iroquois. The French began trading with the Indians they met, including the Iroquois. Beads, metal tools, iron kettles, and eventually guns changed the lives of the Indians. The Dutch and English later settled in what is now New York. These groups' competition with the French led to their making agreements with the Iroquois, which later served to pit the Iroquois against the French and the Huron, who were allied with the French.

By 1600, the united Iroquois had begun their rise to power in the Northeast. After the French teamed up with the Huron, the Iroquois turned to the Dutch as trading partners. In 1614, the Dutch set up a trading post near what would become Fort Orange and established the colony of New Netherland. This trade alliance proved especially valuable after **SMALLPOX**, a disease introduced by Europeans, began killing thousands of Indians in the Northeast. The epidemic of 1633 killed so many Iroquois that they began waging "mourning wars" against neighboring Indian tribes. Instead of harming their war captives, they adopted most of them into their families in hopes of repopulating their diminished clans.

FROM THEIR INITIAL ENTRY POINT ON MANHATTAN ISLAND, DUTCH SETTLERS CLAIMED MORE TRIBAL LANDS UP THE HUDSON RIVER.

FRENCH EXPLORER SAMUEL DE CHAMPLAIN AIDED THE HURON IN EARLY-1600S WARS AGAINST THE IROQUOIS.

When they began trading with the Dutch, the Iroquois made agreements called covenants that tied the Dutch and Iroquois together as tightly as if they had been physically bound by rope. Later, the two sides signed a written treaty. The Iroquois referred to this agreement as a "chain." For more than 100 years, further agreements the Iroquois made with their European neighbors would be called the "Covenant Chain" after these early treaties.

By 1648, the Iroquois were ready to expand their reach. They began a campaign known as the Beaver Wars to destroy their Indian neighbors and take over the fur trade. Armed with guns provided by Dutch traders, the Iroquois attacked their longtime enemies, the Huron. To Europeans who witnessed the fighting, the Iroquois goal was clear. A French **JESUIT** missionary captured by the Iroquois said, "it is the design of the Iroquois to capture all the Huron, put the chiefs and a great part of the nation to death, and with the rest to form one nation and one country." Many of the Huron had been converted to Christianity by the French Jesuit priests who came to their villages and introduced the Christian religion. By 1650, the Iroquois had nearly exterminated the Huron and pushed other tribes farther west. Within the next decade, the Iroquois became the strongest Indian nation in the Northeast.

The Iroquois had always warred with nearby tribes, but guns provided by European traders caused greater loss of life and put tribes on a more equal footing with one another. In 1663, the Iroquois attacked the Susquehannock in Maryland. The Susquehannock, also supplied with Dutch weaponry, refused to surrender. They captured 25 Iroquois peace delegates, forced them

THE IROQUOIS GENERAL ⟶ *The grandson of Red Jacket, a famous Seneca leader, Ely Parker helped* **ANTHROPOLOGIST** *Lewis Henry Morgan compile material for a book about the Iroquois. When the Civil War began in 1861, Parker joined the U.S. Army. He became military secretary to General Ulysses S. Grant. After Grant became president in 1869, he named Parker as his commissioner of Indian affairs. The first Indian to hold this office, Parker grew frustrated at the government's treatment of Indians.*

1842

IROQUOIS

onto scaffolds, and "in sight of their own army, they were burned alive," according to the writings of Jesuit priest Jerome Lalemant.

Contact with the Europeans also proved costly to the Iroquois in other ways—most notably, in exposing the Iroquois to disease. In 1664, a fatal smallpox epidemic struck Iroquois villages. More than 1,000 Iroquois died, and many others fled their villages. Weakened by disease, the Iroquois could now be attacked by neighboring tribes such as the Mahican (or Mohican) and by the French, who set out to eliminate the Iroquois.

Peace with the French in 1667 soon brought Jesuit missionaries to Iroquois villages. As had been their aim with other tribes, the missionaries came to convert the Indians to Christianity. Many Iroquois accepted the new religion and moved into separate villages made up of Christian converts. One of these villages was at Kahnawake in Canada. Some converts, such as **KATERI TEKAKWITHA**, became famous for their loyalty to the new religion. Because of the Catholic Church's ties to the French, some Iroquois then became allies of the French, while others remained friends with the British and Dutch.

Thanks to such divided allegiances, the Iroquois fought on

⇢=== **FROM LACROSSE TO HOLLYWOOD** ===⇠ *Born Harold Smith in Canada, Jay Silverheels was a Canadian Mohawk familiar to a generation of children as Tonto, the Lone Ranger's Indian partner in the 1950s television show* The Lone Ranger. *Silverheels, a skilled* **LACROSSE** *player, came to the U.S. in 1938. He appeared as Geronimo in* Broken Arrow (1950), *a classic film that was among the first to portray Indians as more humane characters. A skilled athlete and activist, he was the first American Indian to receive a star on Hollywood's Walk of Fame.*

both sides of the wars between the French and British. Again finding themselves in danger of losing access to western furs and suffering from a dwindling population after a horrible smallpox epidemic in 1679, the Iroquois battled the French and their Indian allies from 1680 to 1701. In the Ohio River Valley, the Iroquois in 1680 attacked the Miami and Illinois, two tribes who provided furs to the French. They killed 30 people but captured more than 300. These captives were adopted into Iroquois families.

The French started attacking some Iroquois villages in 1687. Their Ojibwa and Abenaki allies joined them in destroying crops and burning Iroquois towns. Many Iroquois starved to death, and many more were forced to flee their homes. By 1700, the Iroquois had lost 20 percent of their population.

As they warred with the French, the Iroquois also faced trouble from the English to the south. William Penn, founder of Pennsylvania, wanted to purchase Indian land to expand his colony. The Lenape/Delaware Indians (inhabitants of eastern Pennsylvania, western New Jersey, and eastern Delaware) became Penn's allies, which angered the Iroquois. In 1701, the Iroquois made a treaty of peace with both the English and the French called

CORNPLANTER
(ABOVE) SAW
ACTION WITH
THE BRITISH IN
REVOLUTIONARY
BATTLES SUCH AS
THOSE REENACTED
TODAY (RIGHT).

the Grand Settlement. If the English and French went to war again, the Iroquois promised to remain neutral.

However, some war chiefs, such as the Seneca leader **CORNPLANTER**, had already allied themselves with the British. When the French and Indian War (1754–63) began, the Seneca and three other Iroquois nations fought with Britain to once and for all oust the French from their rule in North America. With the British now controlling most of the Northeast, it seemed as though the Iroquois might finally enjoy a time of peace.

The outbreak of war between Britain and the American colonists in 1776 forced the Iroquois to make some tough choices. Many Iroquois felt a strong loyalty to Britain. Joseph Brant, a friend and relative of British Indian representative William Johnson, encouraged his fellow Mohawk to side with the British. An American missionary persuaded several of the Oneida and Tuscarora to side with the Americans. For the first time in many years, the Iroquois League became seriously divided.

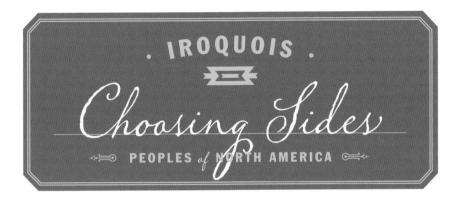

The Iroquois homeland became a battleground during the Revolutionary War. American settlers on the New York and Pennsylvania frontiers saw their homes burned and looted, their crops destroyed, and their families killed as battles swept over the region. General George Washington later sent his armies into the Iroquois homeland to burn villages and drive the Indians off their lands. Many Iroquois fled north to Canada.

When the U.S. Congress gathered in Philadelphia in 1787 to adopt the Constitution, they were influenced by the writings of Benjamin Franklin and Thomas Jefferson. Both statesmen admired the Iroquois and their model of consensus-based, representative government. The Iroquois Great Law of Peace may have inspired American laws on libel (false statements against a person's character), free speech, freedom of religion, freedom from illegal search and seizure, and the system of checks and balances that is supposed to make government run more smoothly.

After the American Revolution, the Iroquois, like many other Indian nations east of the Mississippi River, lost much of their land as settlers moved west. They also let go of much of their traditional culture. Around 1800, a

IN THE 1750S, GEORGE WASHINGTON HAD FOUGHT ALONGSIDE THE SENECA BUT ORDERED "TOTAL DESTRUCTION" OF THEIR VILLAGES IN 1779.

ALTHOUGH NOT THE FIRST AMERICAN CITY TO HOUSE A SKYSCRAPER, NEW YORK BECAME THE MOST EXPERIMENTAL WITH THE FORM.

Seneca leader named **HANDSOME LAKE** tried to recapture the Iroquoian cultural identity in a new religion. It became a mix of traditional rituals and **QUAKER** beliefs. In 1838, the Iroquois signed a treaty that cost them most of their lands in western New York. Most Oneida were moved to a reservation in Wisconsin in 1846. Some Cayuga, Seneca, and Onondaga migrated to Indian Territory (Oklahoma). The Iroquois who remained in New York lived on small reservations.

By the mid-1800s, the Iroquois were being pressured to assimilate, or adopt American culture. Some Iroquois left the reservations to work in cities. Others struggled to make a living as farmers. Although they were not U.S. citizens, many Iroquois enlisted in the U.S. military during the Civil War (1861–65) and World War I (1914–18) and fought heroically to defend the nation. One such Iroquois was Seneca Ely Parker. He served as an officer and assistant to General Ulysses S. Grant during the Civil War.

In 1942, the Iroquois Confederacy declared war on Germany and the Axis Powers, enabling Iroquois men to enlist on the side of the U.S. and the Allies. For many young people, going off to military training was the first time they had left their reservation. At war's end, many young Iroquois moved to cities across the nation and did not return to life on the reservations.

The U.S. government encouraged them to do this through a program called relocation. This practice had begun in the 1880s. In their jobs as ironworkers, many Iroquois had helped build the Empire State Building, the Golden Gate Bridge, the Chrysler Building, the World Trade Center, and dozens of other structures. Many of the Mohawk went to work on America's tallest skyscrapers. Their skills were well known to construction companies. As

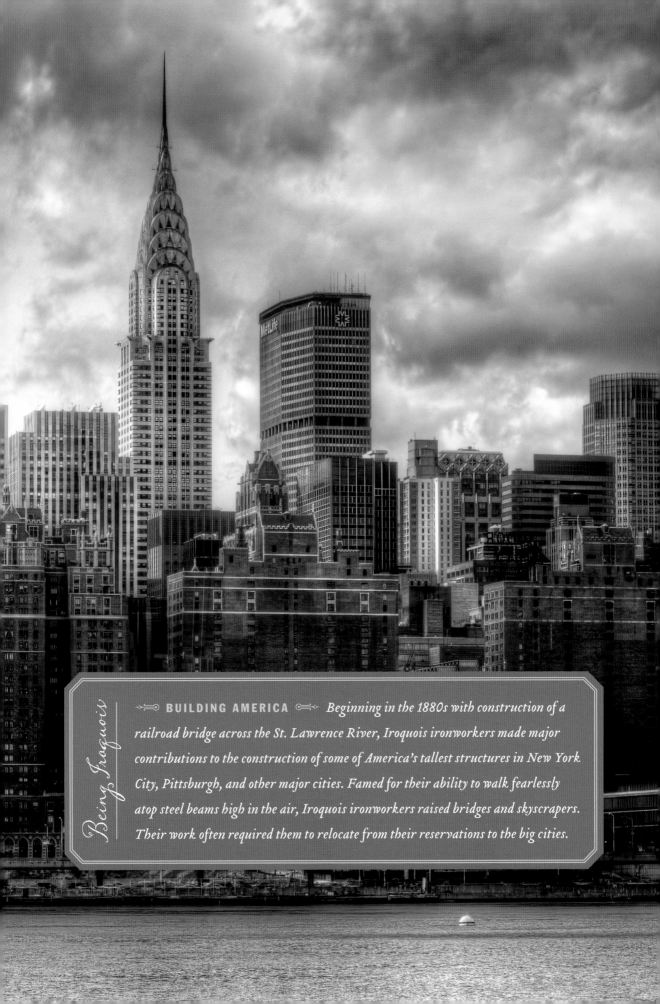

Being Iroquois

⇥ **BUILDING AMERICA** ⇤ _Beginning in the 1880s with construction of a railroad bridge across the St. Lawrence River, Iroquois ironworkers made major contributions to the construction of some of America's tallest structures in New York City, Pittsburgh, and other major cities. Famed for their ability to walk fearlessly atop steel beams high in the air, Iroquois ironworkers raised bridges and skyscrapers. Their work often required them to relocate from their reservations to the big cities._

one foreman at Dominion Bridge Company said, "putting riveting tools in the Mohawk's hands was like putting ham with eggs."

Throughout the last half of the 20th century, the Iroquois faced new challenges. Some leaders in the U.S. Congress pushed for the implementation of a process called termination that would end the federal government's management of the reservations. Promises of help made to the tribes under treaties signed in the 1800s would effectively be considered null and void. Indians would be given full citizenship rights and be held to state laws. More than 100 tribes were terminated between 1953 and 1964, but the Iroquois fought hard to keep their rights. Seneca leader **ALICE JEMISON** told Congress, "We have kept our shares of the treaties, and we are here to ask that you keep yours." Such testimony was powerful enough to save the Iroquois from termination—and their land from private ownership.

The government's quest to dam rivers for irrigation, flood control, and hydropower projects in the 1950s and '60s brought it into conflict with the Iroquois. The Seneca objected to government efforts to dam the Allegheny River. The proposed **KINZUA DAM**, Seneca leaders argued, would flood a tribal cemetery and much of their lands. In this case, the government won. The dam was built, and thousands of acres of reservation land were flooded. Other Iroquois lands were overtaken for New York's interstate system.

The Tuscarora, though, won part of their fight against a dam the government wanted to build on their land. The tribe refused to accept New York state's offer of $3 million for their land and took their fight to Washington, D.C. In 1959, the federal government agreed that the Tuscarora could not be forced to sell their land. About 20 percent of their reservation was taken to make a reservoir for the Niagara power plant, though.

As Indians became active in the civil rights movement of

THE LAKE CREATED BY THE KINZUA DAM— THE ALLEGHENY RES- ERVOIR—STRETCHES NORTH TO THE SENECA RESERVATION IN NEW YORK.

MEMBERS FROM
TRIBES SUCH AS THE
ONONDAGA CON-
TINUE TO REMIND
THE U.S. GOVERN-
MENT OF THEIR
TREATY RIGHTS.

the 1960s and '70s, the Iroquois worked to ensure that the U.S.
government honored other commitments made to the Indians
under treaties. In a 1968 show of protest, the Iroquois barricaded
the Cornwall International Bridge between Canada and the U.S.
According to Jay's Treaty of 1794, the Iroquois were permitted to
move back and forth from Canada to the U.S. without any restric-
tions. Although the U.S. Congress formally recognized this right
again in 1928, the Canadian government had not. After months of
protests, the Canadians agreed in 1969 to honor the treaty. Each
July, the Iroquois hold a Border Crossing Ceremony to remind
both the Canadian and American governments of this treaty right.

As with many Indian nations, the Iroquois today struggle to
find their place in American society. More and more children attend off-reservation schools and then completely leave the reservation for college. This trend has led to a serious decline in the
number of Iroquois who still speak their native languages and

⟶ CONSCIENCE OF A NATION ⟵ *Oren Lyons (pictured as honorary chairman of the Iroquois Nationals) is a champion lacrosse player, commercial artist, college professor, activist, and Faithkeeper of the Turtle Clan of the Seneca. After playing lacrosse in college and for several professional teams, Lyons became a commercial artist in New York City. In 1970, he returned to the Onondaga reservation in northern New York. He was active in the Indian civil rights movement of the 1970s and continues to protect native peoples' rights. He is also an author and illustrator of many books.*

preserve the ancient traditions.

As the Iroquois assimilate further into American culture, some Iroquois leaders worry that traditional beliefs will disappear entirely. However, Oren Lyons, Faithkeeper of the Seneca Nation, is confident his people's beliefs will survive: "The elders said, 'As long as there's one [Iroquois] to sing and one to dance, one to speak and one to listen, life will go on.'"

One practice sure to continue is the independent sovereignty of the Iroquois nation—in government and in sport. The Iroquois Nationals is a lacrosse team that competes in international meets. Lacrosse is a sport that originated with the Iroquois. In 1987, the International Lacrosse Federation recognized the Iroquois Nationals as an independent team just like those of other nations such as the U.S., Britain, and Canada. When the Nationals team members travel, they use passports granted by the Iroquois Confederacy. Countries around the world now recognize the Iroquois Confederacy as a sovereign nation.

THE IROQUOIS NATIONALS HAVE PARTNERED WITH NIKE SINCE 2006 TO "PROMOTE WELLNESS AND FITNESS" IN NATIVE COMMUNITIES.

*The earliest Iroquois origin stories were recorded by Europeans
in about 1632. The following story explains how the earth and its
plants, flowers, and moon came to exist. Like many origin stories, it describes animals and powerful beings that are central to
Iroquois culture.*

Before our world began, humans lived in SkyWorld. Below
SkyWorld was a dark, watery world with birds and swim-
ming animals. In SkyWorld was the Celestial Tree from
which all kinds of fruits and flowers grew. The Chief of SkyWorld's
wife was Skywoman. One night, the pregnant Skywoman dreamed
that the Celestial Tree was uprooted. When she told her husband
about it, he realized they needed to do everything they could to
make it come true.

Many young men in SkyWorld tried to uproot the tree but failed.
Finally, the Chief wrapped his arms around the tree and with
one pull uprooted it. This left a great hole in SkyWorld's crust.
Skywoman leaned over to look into the hole, lost her balance, and
fell in. As she slipped, she grasped a handful of seeds from the
Celestial Tree's branches.

The birds and animals in the water below saw Skywoman tumble
and realized she would not be able to survive in the water. Geese
flew up and caught her between their wings and began to lower
her. Each animal dove into the water, trying to bring up enough
earth from the bottom for Skywoman to land on. When it seemed
as though all had tried and failed, tiny Muskrat vowed to bring up
earth or die trying. She went down deep, deep, deep, until she was
almost unconscious but was able to reach out with one small paw
and grasp some earth before floating back to the top. When Muskrat

appeared, Great Turtle said the pile of earth could be placed on his back. Once there, it began to spread until it became the whole world.

The geese gently set Skywoman on the earth, and she opened her hands to let the seeds fall on the soil. From the seeds grew the trees and grass, and life on Earth had begun.

In time, Skywoman gave birth to Tekawerahkwa, who grew to be a lovely young woman. A powerful being called West Wind fell in love with Tekawerahkwa and took her as his bride. She then gave birth to twin sons.

One (Bad Mind) had skin as hard as flint and was argumentative, and the other (Good Mind) was soft-skinned and patient. While his gentle brother was being born the natural way, Bad Mind forced his way out through his mother's armpit, killing her. When Skywoman asked her grandsons who had done this awful thing, Bad Mind blamed Good Mind. Skywoman banished Good Mind from Earth. Skywoman placed her daughter's head in the night sky where she became Grandmother Moon and was given power over the waters. From her body grew our Three Sisters corn, beans, and squash.

Fortunately, Grandfather came to Good Mind's aid. He taught Good Mind how to make the land beautiful. Good Mind created rivers, mountains, and trees. He taught birds to sing and water animals to dance. He made rainbows and soft rains. Bad Mind was envious. He created the opposite of all his good brother had made.

One day, Bad Mind stole all the animals and hid them in a big cave. A tiny mouse told Good Mind what his brother had done. Good Mind went to the cave and caused the mountain to shake until it split. He fought his brother, using a deer antler as a weapon. When Good Mind finally won, he banished Bad Mind to live in caves, where he waits to return one day.

ALICE JEMISON
(1901–64) Iroquois activist who gave voice to widespread criticism of the Bureau of Indian Affairs in the 1930s and opposed termination of reservation status in the 1940s and '50s

ANTHROPOLOGIST
someone who studies the physical traits, cultures, and relationships of different peoples

CORNPLANTER
(c. 1732–1836) Seneca war chief who supported the British during the American Revolution but afterward signed treaties giving Indian lands to the U.S. government. He was granted about 1,500 acres (607 ha), known as Cornplanter's Tract, of former Seneca land in Pennsylvania, which was flooded by the Kinzua Dam in 1965

DEGANAWIDA
considered a prophet among the Iroquois and known as "The Great Peacemaker," Deganawida and his follower Hiawatha founded the initial Iroquois Confederacy of five nations

GREAT LAW OF PEACE
the oral, or spoken, constitution for a code of behavior brought to the Iroquois by Deganawida and Hiawatha in the mid-1500s; the 117 articles of law were first recorded through wampum belts and later translated into English

HANDSOME LAKE
(1735–1815) the half-brother of Cornplanter, Handsome Lake was a religious prophet who encouraged the Iroquois to return to their traditional ceremonies, work to build and protect their families, and ban alcohol

JESUIT
a Catholic priest belonging to the Society of Jesus, a group dedicated to missionary outreach and educational efforts on behalf of the Catholic Church

KATERI TEKAKWITHA
(1656–80) known as the "Lily of the Mohawks," Kateri was born to a Christian mother and died of smallpox at a Catholic mission near Montreal, Quebec; the Catholic Church attributed miracles to her, and she was canonized (made a saint) in October 2012

KINZUA DAM
finished in 1965, the dam covered a large part of the Allegany Reservation, the Seneca homeland in New York promised to Cornplanter in 1794

LACROSSE
a popular sport that originated with an Iroquois game; played with sticks and a wooden ball about the size of a grapefruit, the objective is to get the ball into the opposing side's net

LONGHOUSE
ranging from 20 to 150 feet (6.1–45.7 m) long and 15 to 25 feet (4.6–7.6 m) wide, the longhouse was built using sheets of basswood or elm bark corded to upright poles and bent into an arch

QUAKER
having to do with the Quakers, a Christian group that emphasizes individual worship of God and peaceful practices; Quakers were especially active in Pennsylvania, near the Iroquois of Handsome Lake's time

SMALLPOX
a contagious disease that causes fever and skin blisters

WAMPUM
beads cut from the shells of sea mollusks such as whelk and quahog clam; they were ground, polished, and drilled through the center to be strung together or woven onto objects

Abler, Thomas S. *Cornplanter: Chief Warrior of the Allegany Senecas.* Syracuse, N.Y.: Syracuse University Press, 2007.

Grumet, Robert S., ed. *Northeastern Indian Lives, 1632–1816.* Amherst: University of Massachusetts Press, 1996.

Jennings, Francis. *The Ambiguous Iroquois Empire.* New York: W. W. Norton, 1984.

Johnson, Michael G. *Iroquois: People of the Longhouse.* Buffalo, N.Y.: Firefly Books, 2013.

Richter, Daniel K. *The Ordeal of the Longhouse: The Peoples of the Iroquois League in the Era of European Colonization.* Chapel Hill: University of North Carolina Press, 1992.

Richter, Daniel K., and James H. Merrell, eds. *Beyond the Covenant Chain: The Iroquois and Their Neighbors in Indian North America, 1600–1800.* Syracuse, N.Y.: Syracuse University Press, 1987.

Snow, Dean R. *The Iroquois.* Cambridge, Mass.: Blackwell, 1996.

Trigger, Bruce, ed. *Northeast.* Vol. 15 of *Handbook of North American Indians*, edited by William C. Sturtevant. Washington, D.C.: Smithsonian Institution, 1978.

Wallace, Anthony F. C. *The Death and Rebirth of the Seneca.* New York: Knopf, 1969.

⇢⇒ READ MORE ⇐⇠

Bjornlund, Lydia. *The Iroquois.* San Diego: Lucent, 2001.

Bolton, Jonathan, and Claire Wilson. *Joseph Brant: Mohawk Chief.* New York: Chelsea House, 1992.

⇢⇒ WEBSITES ⇐⇠

CARNEGIE MUSEUM OF NATURAL HISTORY: IROQUOIS OF THE NORTHEAST
http://carnegiemnh.org/online/indians/iroquois /index.html
Learn more about Iroquois history and culture.

IROQUOIS INDIAN MUSEUM
http://www.iroquoismuseum.org/
Explore how works of art relate to aspects of Iroquois life.